WHAT WE GET FROM CELTIC MYTHOLOGY

KATIE MARSICO

CHERRY LAKE

Publishing

Published in the United States of America
by Cherry Lake Publishing
Ann Arbor, Michigan
www.cherrylakepublishing.com

Consultants: Lesley Jacobs, Mellon Postdoctoral Fellow in English, Brown University; Marla Conn, ReadAbility, Inc.
Editorial direction and book production: Red Line Editorial

Photo Credits: Brendan Donnelly/Demotix/Corbis, cover, 1; Shutterstock Images, 5, 6; CM Dixon/Heritage Images/Glow Images, 9; Joseph Christian Leyendecker, 11 (left); Stapleton Collection/Corbis, 11 (right); Public Domain, 13, 18; North Wind Picture Archives, 15; Lian Deng/Shutterstock Images, 17; Matthew Ashton/AMA/Corbis, 21; Edmund Blair Leighton, 23; Mat Hayward/Shutterstock Images, 24; Columbia Pictures/Everett Collection, 27; Everett Collection/Glow Images, 28 (left); Bettmann/Corbis, 28 (right)

Library of Congress Cataloging-in-Publication Data

Marsico, Katie, 1980- author.
  What we get from Celtic mythology / by Katie Marsico.
    pages cm. -- (Mythology and culture)
  Includes index.
  ISBN 978-1-63188-910-3 (hardcover : alk. paper) -- ISBN 978-1-63188-926-4 (pbk. : alk. paper) -- ISBN 978-1-63188-942-4 (pdf) -- ISBN 978-1-63188-958-5 (hosted ebook)
 1. Mythology, Celtic--Juvenile literature. 2. Civilization, Celtic--Influence--Juvenile literature. I. Title.

  BL900.M4625 2015
  398.2089'916--dc23

                    2014029987

Cherry Lake Publishing would like to acknowledge the work of
The Partnership for 21st Century Skills. Please visit *www.p21.org*
for more information.

Printed in the United States of America
Corporate Graphics
December 2014

ABOUT THE AUTHOR

Katie Marsico has written more than 150 reference books for children and young adults. Before becoming a writer, Marsico worked as an editor in Chicago, Illinois. She lives in a suburb of that city with her husband and five children.

TABLE OF CONTENTS

CHAPTER 1

EUROPEAN MYTHS 4

CHAPTER 2

ASTOUNDING STORIES 8

CHAPTER 3

HOW LEGENDS LIVE ON.............14

CHAPTER 4

FROM PAINTINGS
TO PUNK ROCK.........................20

CHAPTER 5

MYTHS AND MOVIEMAKING......26

THINK ABOUT IT 30
LEARN MORE..31
GLOSSARY..32
INDEX...32

EUROPEAN MYTHS

The lush landscape of Western Europe was the original scenery for the Celtic people. Today's culture is still strongly influenced by their rich and exciting past. As early as 600 BCE, the Greeks wrote about the people who lived in these areas. These people would later become known as Celts. The Celts originally lived in Western Europe but later moved westward into the British Isles. Two main groups of languages, Gaelic and Brythonic, developed there. Gaelic languages trace back

Reconstructions of Celtic houses at archaeological sites show visitors how the ancient Celts lived.

to Scotland, Ireland, and the Isle of Man. Brythonic languages originated in Wales, Cornwall, and Brittany.

Besides language, another important part of Celtic culture is its colorful **mythology**. The Celts told fantastic tales of fierce warriors, legendary kings, and **romantic tragedies**. They also told stories of a **supernatural** otherworld that was filled with fairies, mystical cauldrons, and shape-changing animals. Early Celts worshiped many gods and goddesses.

By the 200s BCE, Celtic culture had spread to what is now Turkey. Ancient Celts farmed the land, built impressive forts, and created settlements. A king typically headed each tribe. Tribes included different

THE BRITISH ISLES AND BRITTANY

social classes. One class contained knights and warriors. Another was made up of religious leaders called druids. Druids acted as trusted advisers and respected teachers. Farmers and working people formed a third class.

Between 225 BCE and 84 CE, the Celts were pushed westward by warring armies, including Roman and **Germanic** forces. Few written records of Celtic mythology exist from before that period. The druids' religious rules forbade them from writing down many of their beliefs. Instead, information was passed down through storytelling.

As a result, some of the earliest accounts of Celtic culture come from Roman invaders. Christian monks in Ireland and Wales began recording local **myths** in the 700s. Thanks to their efforts and hundreds of years of storytelling, Celtic mythology lives on today.

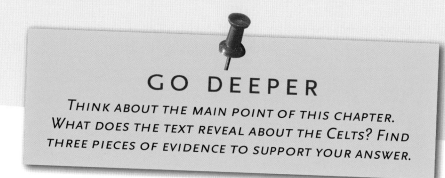

GO DEEPER

THINK ABOUT THE MAIN POINT OF THIS CHAPTER. WHAT DOES THE TEXT REVEAL ABOUT THE CELTS? FIND THREE PIECES OF EVIDENCE TO SUPPORT YOUR ANSWER.

ASTOUNDING STORIES

Celtic myths offer a glimpse into an exciting world in which fact and fantasy often blur. Sometimes the characters and stories that make up Celtic mythology are linked to real-life people and events. In other cases, they are shaped by ideas about magic and the supernatural.

Early Celtic mythology also features the Tuatha Dé Danann. This race of people with supernatural powers plays an important part in the mythology. Before Christianity became widespread, the Celts worshiped

[21ST CENTURY SKILLS LIBRARY]

Experts believe images on Celtic artifacts may depict Celtic myths and gods.

these beings as gods. Several stories about the Tuatha Dé Danann appear in the Mythological Cycle. This is the first cycle, or collection of stories, within early Irish mythology.

The Mythological Cycle provides a fictional account of Ireland's ancient history. The Tuatha Dé Danann are said to be among the first settlers of Ireland. A god called the Dagda is usually viewed as their leader. Celtic myths depict him as a strong warrior with a gigantic club. One end of this weapon is used to kill. The other end restores life. The Dagda also owns a magical cauldron. This pot produces endless food.

The next cycle in early Irish mythology is the Ulster Cycle. It tells of the Ulaid, a group of people living in northeastern Ireland. Most Ulster myths take place in the first century BCE. Several myths feature a character named Cú Chulainn.

Some experts compare Cú Chulainn to Hercules and Achilles, who were famous warriors from Roman and Greek mythology. Like them, Cú Chulainn has a **divine** parent. His mother is human, but his father is Lúg, the Celtic god of sun and light. Lúg is also a member of the Tuatha Dé Danann.

In addition to being half-divine, Cú Chulainn is handsome and athletic. He is extremely fierce in combat, too. One Ulster myth describes Cú Chulainn as an expert swimmer since the day he was born. Another involves him killing a vicious dog with his bare hands at the age of seven.

Fionn MacCumhaill, also called Finn McCool, is another Celtic mythological hero. He is often portrayed as a giant. He is the central figure within the next cycle of stories, the Fenian Cycle. These Irish myths are set in

LOOK AGAIN

Look at these modern illustrations of Cú Chulainn, left, and Achilles, right. What do you notice about each mythological hero? How are they alike and how are they different?

the 200s CE. Several Fenian legends focus on Fionn's leadership of a band of warriors called the Fianna. The stories show him overcoming several challenges to gain wisdom and respect.

The Brythonic myths include some of the first descriptions of the legendary British leader King Arthur. Historians still aren't sure whether Arthur truly existed. They suspect that if he did, he lived in the 400s CE. At that point, the Celtic leaders of post-Roman Britain were battling Germanic invaders.

One well-known Brythonic myth is the tragic romance of Tristan and Isolde. Tristan is the nephew of King Mark of Cornwall. He travels to Ireland on his uncle's behalf to bring back King Mark's future bride, Princess Isolde. Yet she and Tristan fall in love after drinking a magical potion. Later, Tristan is fatally wounded by a spear. Isolde dies of a broken heart.

Later folk customs of Celtic-language speakers brought new details to the mythology, including an

*In this modern illustration, Fionn MacCumhaill
arrives to lead the Fianna.*

array of magical creatures. Among them were fairies,
spirits, goblins, and banshees. Wizards and witches are
also found in Celtic mythology. So are beasts such as
kelpies and selkies. In Celtic legends, kelpies are water
demons that resemble horses. Selkies look like seals
when they swim. On land they take human form. Many
of these creatures and characters can still be seen in
modern culture.

How Legends Live On

Celtic mythology has endured the test of time. Its colorful characters and important ideas have left a powerful cultural **legacy**. They have shaped modern myths and centuries of famous literature. In some cases, their influence isn't immediately obvious. Yet it is still there.

For example, people outside of Ireland are not always familiar with the Tuatha Dé Danann. This is partly because the identity of these gods changed as Christianity spread throughout Europe during the

The arrival of Christianity in Ireland led to changes in the identities of the old Celtic gods.

Middle Ages between the 400s and the 1400s. Christians believe in one God, so Irish monks avoided referring to the Celtic gods as actual **deities**.

During the late 1800s and early 1900s, the Tuatha Dé Danann played a role in the Irish Celtic Revival. This was a literary movement heavily based in Irish history and mythology. In 1904, Irish author Lady Augusta Gregory published *Gods and Fighting Men*. The book is a retelling of a collection of Celtic legends, including stories about the Tuatha Dé Danann. More than a century later, these retellings continue to hold a place in Irish folklore. According to some legends, members of the Tuatha Dé Danann are the ancestors of leprechauns. These mischievous fairies are world-famous symbols of Ireland and Irish mythology.

It is also possible that Celtic myths are at the heart of well-known legends surrounding the Scottish lake called Loch Ness. In 1933, people began reporting sightings of a mysterious beast in the lake. It became known as the Loch Ness Monster. Stories about Loch Ness often refer to the water-dwelling creatures called kelpies that appear throughout Celtic mythology.

The Irish Celtic Revival also breathed new life into the Ulster and Fenian cycles. Fionn MacCumhaill is a central character in James Stephens's *Irish Fairy Tales*. This collection of folklore was published in 1920. In it, Stephens retells Fenian myths.

Like Fionn and Cú Chulainn, the character of King Arthur has become immortal, too. Adventure, love, and

In the 1900s, the huge lake known as Loch Ness became linked with kelpies, creatures from Celtic mythology.

chivalry are important themes within this type of storytelling. Beginning in the 1100s, French authors crafted new Arthurian romances. They also described Camelot. This is the mythical location of Arthur's palace and court.

Writers started weaving tales about other Arthurian characters as well. These characters include the sorcerer Merlin, a knight named Sir Lancelot, and Arthur's wife,

King Arthur is one of the most famous characters of Celtic mythology.

Guinevere. In addition, Arthurian romances refer to the king's mythical sword, Excalibur. Several of the romances describe his quest for a mythical cup known as the Holy Grail.

Between 1842 and 1888, British poet Alfred, Lord Tennyson revisited these images. He wrote a collection of poems titled *Idylls of the King*. Tennyson's work mentions Arthur's dream of creating an ideal kingdom based on peace, justice, and equality. Today, both Arthur and Camelot remain symbols of chivalry and people's efforts to build a better world.

Tristan and Isolde are also referenced in *Idylls of the King*. The theme of doomed lovers was revisited in several later works, including William Shakespeare's play *Romeo and Juliet*. People often credit the Celtic myth with paving the way for other famous romantic tragedies.

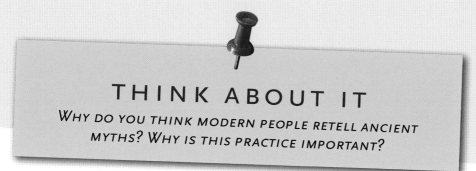

THINK ABOUT IT
WHY DO YOU THINK MODERN PEOPLE RETELL ANCIENT MYTHS? WHY IS THIS PRACTICE IMPORTANT?

CHAPTER 4

FROM PAINTINGS TO PUNK ROCK

Language and artifacts, or historical objects, have also kept Celtic mythology alive. The same is true of art and music. References to myths still exist in expressions used in everyday speech. This is especially true in Celtic nations.

For example, the Irish often refer to Cú Chulainn's physical strength and skill. In the hero's legendary origin, "Setanta" is his birth name. He later changes it to Cú Chulainn. The name Setanta appears in the names of several Irish athletic clubs.

Meanwhile, the phrase "wail like a banshee" is well known in many parts of the English-speaking world. It describes loud crying or screaming. In Irish folklore, a banshee shrieks nearby just before a person dies.

The name Setanta *has lived on in an Irish sports-broadcasting company.*

Many historical artifacts also contain reminders of Celtic mythology. These objects include coins, jewelry, shields, helmets, tapestries, and metalwork. One famous example is the Gundestrup cauldron. This silver pot may date back to 200 BCE. Some of the images on the cauldron depict scenes similar to those in the Celtic myths.

Roughly 2,000 years later, Herbert James Draper and Jack Butler Yeats captured the spirit of Celtic myths in their paintings. Artists such as Edmund Blair Leighton, Frederic Leighton, and Hugues Merle did the same. Some of their masterpieces depict mythological creatures, including kelpies. Others show Tristan and Isolde or scenes of Arthurian romance.

Celtic mythology lives on in songs and stage productions, too. In 1865, an opera based on the story of Tristan and Isolde story premiered in Munich, Germany. Composer Richard Wagner's emotional

LOOK AGAIN

This painting by Edmund Blair Leighton shows Tristan and Isolde. What can you tell about the characters and the story based on looking at the painting?

Even rock bands, such as the Dropkick Murphys, have made use of Celtic mythology.

presentation of the tragic Celtic romance became known for bringing people to tears.

More recently, rock 'n' roll artists have found inspiration in the life of Fionn MacCumhaill. In 2001, the song "The Legend of Finn MacCumhail" was featured on an album by the Dropkick Murphys.

The band is an American group that plays what is known as Celtic punk rock. This kind of music blends rock music with traditional Celtic music. The following lyrics summarize Fionn's legacy, using an English version of his name: "Known as a hero to all that he knew, long live the legend of Finn MacCuil! The brave fearless leader of the chosen few, long live the legend of Finn MacCuil!" In 2010, the musical *Finn McCool* debuted in Washington, DC. It also relies on punk rock to retell Fenian mythology.

Myths and Moviemaking

The entertainment industry has also helped Celtic mythology spread and survive. These tales continue to reach audiences in the form of films.

Many famous movies rooted in Celtic myths feature King Arthur. They include animated films such as *The Sword in the Stone* and *Quest for Camelot. Monty Python and the Holy Grail* is a comedic retelling of Arthurian legends. Other movies based on the King Arthur legend include *Excalibur, The Mists of Avalon, King Arthur,* and *Camelot.*

The film The Water Horse *features a beast inspired by the Celtic kelpie and the Loch Ness Monster.*

Hollywood producers have retold more than Arthurian myths. In 2006, actors James Franco and Sophia Myles appeared in the film *Tristan + Isolde*. In 2012, actor Michael Fassbender declared his plans to develop a movie about Cú Chulainn.

Other productions feature mythological creatures related to Celtic mythology. *Darby O'Gill and the Little People* is a family film about leprechauns. These fairies are also the subject of the horror movie *Leprechaun*. Moviemakers have portrayed kelpies and selkies onscreen as well. Myths about such beasts appear in *The Secret of Roan Inish, The Water Horse,* and *Ondine.*

LOOK AGAIN

Look at these depictions of King Arthur. How are they similar? How are they different?

[21ST CENTURY SKILLS LIBRARY]

These movies are proof of the enduring legacy of Celtic myths. Celtic mythology has given the world heroes, monsters, and legendary leaders. It has provided us with tales of magic, romance, strength, and sorrow. Such myths are often ancient. Yet the stories and their themes continue to speak to contemporary people. They will continue to shape modern cultures for generations to come.

THINK ABOUT IT

- You have read how certain Celtic myths blend fact and fantasy. Why do you think storytellers create fictional versions of actual people and events? Why do you think authors sometimes add or change details when they retell myths?

- Are you familiar with myths from any other cultures? If so, how do they compare to the tales found within Celtic mythology? Do you notice any similarities between themes or characters?

- Visit a reliable Web site to learn more about Celtic mythology. Are you able to find stories describing other mythological heroes? What about other romantic tragedies? How do these myths compare to the tales you read in this book?

LEARN MORE

FURTHER READING

Leavy, Una, and Susan Field (illustrator). *The O'Brien Book of Irish Fairy Tales and Legends*. Dublin, Ireland: O'Brien Press, 2011.

Macdonald, Fiona. *Celtic Myths and Legends*. Chicago, IL: Raintree, 2014.

WEB SITES

Irish Myths and Legends
http://www.theemeraldisle.org/irish-myths-legends
Visit this Web site to read Celtic myths that developed in Ireland.

Iron Age Celts
http://www.bbc.co.uk/wales/celts
Explore this Web site for stories, crafts, and games related to Celtic culture in Wales.

GLOSSARY

chivalry (SHIH-vuhl-ree) an honorable and polite way of behaving, especially toward women

deities (DEE-uh-tees) gods

divine (duh-VINE) of, from, or like a god

Germanic (juhr-MAH-nik) of or relating to Germany

legacy (LEG-uh-see) something handed down from the past

mythology (mih-THOL-uh-jee) a collection of myths dealing with a culture's gods or heroes

myths (MITHS) stories that attempt to describe the origin of a people's customs or beliefs or to explain mysterious events

romantic tragedies (roh-MAN-tik TRA-juh-deez) literary works often involving one or more characters that suffer or die for love

supernatural (soo-puhr-NAH-chuh-ruhl) something better explained by magic or spirituality than science or the laws of nature

INDEX

Arthur, King, 12, 16–19, 26, 28

banshees, 13, 21–22
British Isles, 4–6

Christianity, 7–8, 14–15
Cú Chulainn, 10–11, 16, 20, 27

Dagda, the, 9
druids, 6–7

Fenian Cycle, 12, 16, 25

Greeks, 4, 10

kelpies, 13, 16, 22, 27
kings, 5

leprechauns, 16, 27
Loch Ness Monster, the, 16

MacCumhaill, Fionn, 10, 12, 16, 25
movies, 26–27

music, 22, 24–25
Mythological Cycle, 9

paintings, 22–23

Romans, 7, 10

Tristan and Isolde, 12, 19, 22–24, 27
Tuatha Dé Danann, 8–10, 14–16

Ulster Cycle, 10, 16